THE AUTHORIZED BOLSHOI BALLET BOOK OF
RAYMONDA

THE AUTHORIZED BOLSHOI BALLET BOOK OF
RAYMONDA

By Yuri Grigorovich and Victor Vanslow
Translated by Alexander Kroll

Photography by Vladimir Pchalkin
Captions by Dr. Herbert R. Axelrod

Published through the cooperation of VAAP Copyright Agency of the Soviet Union.

Distributed in the UNITED STATES by T.F.H. Publications, Inc., 211 West Sylvania Avenue, Neptune City, NJ 07753; in CANADA to the Book Trade by Macmillan of Canada (A Division of Canada Publishing Corporation), 164 Commander Boulevard, Agincourt, Ontario M1S 3C7; in ENGLAND by T.F.H. Publications Limited, 4 Kier Park, Ascot, Berkshire SL5 7DS; in AUSTRALIA AND THE SOUTH PACIFIC by T.F.H. (Australia) Pty. Ltd., Box 149, Brookvale 2100 N.S.W., Australia; in NEW ZEALAND by Ross Haines & Son, Ltd., 18 Monmouth Street, Grey Lynn, Auckland 2, New Zealand; in SINGAPORE AND MALAYSIA by MPH Distributors (S) Pte., Ltd., 601 Sims Drive, #03/07/21, Singapore 1438; in the PHILIPPINES by Bio-Research, 5 Lippay Street, San Lorenzo Village, Makati Rizal; in SOUTH AFRICA by Multipet Pty. Ltd., 30 Turners Avenue, Durban 4001. Published by T.F.H. Publications, Inc. Manufactured in the United States of America by T.F.H. Publications, Inc.

CONTENTS

Preface

Glazunov's ballet *Raymonda*, staged by Petipa, belongs among the outstanding creations of musical and choreographic art. It became one of the highlights in the creative work of both the composer and the choreographer. Their cooperation produced wonderful results: The wedding of Glazunov's music to the choreography of the ballet by Petipa produced genuine masterpieces of the art of dance which will live forever. Trivial, even weak in its dramatic composition the libretto was greatly enriched by the lively, full-blooded music and vivid picturesque choreography. *Raymonda* thus became the memorable story of faithful love, the beauty of life and its victory over perfidy, self-love, and malice.

The first presentation by Petipa wasn't all perfect in spite of remarkable achievements. Later other choreographers would try to improve on it; sometimes they succeeded in certain respects but only when they preserved the immortal basis of Petipa.

I knew *Raymonda* when I was a child; I liked the ballet immensely, danced in it. But as a choreographer I couldn't for a long time impel myself to work at it. Only after having accumulated experience in staging new classical ballets did I turn to *Raymonda* with the aim of keeping all the best of Petipa and adding choreography in the same style as his masterpieces. This could be done only on the basis of deepening the general art concept of the play and constructing it on the suite-symphonic principle which produced such brilliant results in Petipa's ensembles and large dancing compositions.

In this book readers will find the analysis of the music and choreography of *Raymonda*, the history of its creation and staging, the analysis of my production. It will put ballet lovers closer to understanding the masterpiece of world choreography.

Moscow
Yuri Grigorovich

Facing page: Yuri Grigorovich, 1987.

Alexander Glazunov (left) with Rimsky-Korsakov.

Chapter I

Glazunov: Classic Master of Russian Music

The *First Symphony* by Alexander Glazunov, an unknown at the time, was performed at a concert in St. Petersburg more than a century ago on March 17, 1882. The audience liked the symphony. They were very surprised and delighted to see a sixteen-year-old youth in the uniform of the "Real" or "Modern School" responding to their applause. Thus Glazunov won appreciation early and rapidly and it followed him all his creative life.

Alexander Konstantinovich Glazunov was born into the family of a publisher on July 29, 1865. The composer lived almost all his life in St. Petersburg (Leningrad) in the same house in which he was born, seldom leaving it for foreign countries. But the real biography of an artist is his creative work which is the history of his spirit and that of his contemporaries and his epoch. And in this respect the composer's biography is full of creative achievements which left a remarkable trace in the world art.

Though Glazunov's parents were not professional musicians they were very musical: his father played the violin, his mother—the piano, and she even studied music theory with M. A. Balakirev and N. A. Rimsky-Korsakov. This acquaintance played a decisive part in the formation of the composer. He began the study of music at the age of eight; at the age of thirteen he became acquainted with Balakirev who, realizing the boy's uncommon talent, called him "Little Glinka." Balakirev recommended that he study privately with Rimsky-Korsakov, under whose guidance he completed a course of composition and theory. These lessons gave birth to his *First Symphony*. Its memorable performance introduced a brilliant new name into Russian musical culture.

His creative work developed rapidly, with many new large instrumental works, each becoming an object of active interest to both the public and musicians.

After leaving the "Real" or modern school Glazunov attended some lectures at the philological department of the university of St. Petersburg. But his self-education was active, voracious and continuous.

Glazunov at 26 years of age.

In 1899 Glazunov was appointed professor at the St. Petersburg Conservatory and in 1905 he became director and held the post until 1928 when ill health made it necessary to go abroad for medical treatment. He died in Paris on March 21, 1936.

In 1972 the remains of the composer were transported from Paris to the Soviet Union and reinterred at the cemetery-necropolis near the graves of other great Russian composers.

Glazunov's creative heritage is enormous. He wrote eight symphonies (the ninth was not completed), five instrumental concertos (among which the concerto for violin with orchestra is the most popular one), a large number of one-part symphonic compositions. Glazunov enriched Russian chamber-instrumental literature by his string ensembles (seven quartets, a quintet, suites), piano sonatas and variations, preludes with fugues for piano and for organ, pieces and ensembles for different instruments.

Vocal music did not attract Glazunov, thus he wrote very few operas, cantatas or oratorios and his few romances were not impressive works. But he is at his best in ballets.

His three ballets all belong to the mature period of his creativity. They appeared on the verge of the 19th-20th centuries when the development of Russian classical ballet reached its culmination. They are: *Raymonda* (1898),

Ruses d'amour (1900), *The Seasons* (1900). These latter two are one-act ballets.

Glazunov is a composer of a vivid original style and this style elaborated first in his symphonic music showed itself to its full extent in his ballets.

What is the essence of his style?

His music is full of optimism, it is closely connected with folksongs. Simple, intelligible and clear—his music is perfect in form. It glorifies the beauty and greatness of man, tells about the joy of life, about the transient character of grief and suffering. It glorifies the immense vastness and the beauty of Russia's fields and rivers.

Glazunov's orchestra always sounds magnificent, rich, even luxurious. His instrumentation reminds one of a multicolored carpet and is characterized by sensuous beauty, light and clear sound. A movement of large sound masses in the orchestra, plasticity, smoothness and gradual changes predominate.

Here is what outstanding soviet musicologist academician B. V. Asafiev said about Glazunov's music: "A spring overflow of a deep river—is an image corresponding to many sound conceptions of this composer." "A thickset, leafy, many-branched oak, with a broad trunk, its roots deep in the ground, firmly connected with it forever—this is one more image which involuntarily appears when you start thinking of Glazunov's sound conceptions. Self-control, conciseness, shortness are not characteristic of his music. Violent impetuousness, flights, rises—but for rare exceptions are not typical of it either."

We don't usually find violent passions or spiritual instability in Glazunov's compositions. His music flows quietly, smoothly, leisurely. It is always balanced, well-proportioned, beautiful.

It is rare when Glazunov's music contains images of sadness or sometimes even gloomy speculations, or violent impetuosity. But such a mood is always overcome in the process of music development and is never a basic point of his principle concepts. By their contrast they underline only more strongly the life-asserting force, the joy of life.

Glazunov's music is more meditative, static, passive than for example the music by Tchaikovsky. He tells more about the joys of the victory, about its wonderful fruit than about the struggle which led to this victory. He erects wonderful buildings; he plants gardens and parks on land which has already been won and only seldom mentions the sacrifices necessary to obtain this beauty.

Enriching and developing musical ways and methods elaborated by Russian classics, Glazunov is not a composer-innovator primarily, but a composer who completes the whole epoch of the development of Russian classical music.

ВЪ МАРІИНСКОМЪ ТЕАТРѢ

Въ Среду, 7-го Января,

ВЪ БЕНЕФИСЪ

Г-жи ПЬЕРИНЫ ЛЕНЬЯНИ

Артистами Императорскихъ театровъ представлено будетъ:

Въ 1-й разъ:

РАЙМОНДА

Балетъ въ 3-хъ дѣйствіяхъ (4-хъ картинахъ). (Сюжетъ заимствованъ изъ рыцарской легенды), сочин. Г-жи Л. Пашковой.

Музыка А. К. Глазунова.

Танцы и постановка балетмейстера М. И. Петипа.

Новыя декораціи: 1-го дѣйствія, 1-й картины—Г. Аллегри, 1-го дѣйствія, 2-й картины, 3-го дѣйствія и пролога—Г. Ламбина, 2-го дѣйствія—Г. Иванова. Машинистъ—Г. Бергеръ. Костюмы женскіе—г-жи Офицеровой, мужскіе—г. Каффи. Головные уборы женскіе—г-жи Тернова, мужскіе—г. Брюно. Аксессуарами зав. В. В. Каменскаго. Парики и прически—г. Педдеръ. Обувь—г-жи Левшицкая. Металлическія вещи—г. Матвѣевъ Трунъ—г-жа Добровольской. Цвѣты—г-жа Ренисовъ.

Роль „Раймонды", исп. Г-жа Пьерина Леньяни.

Дѣйствующія лица:

Раймонда, графиня де-Дорисъ	Г-жа Леньяни
Графиня Сибилла, каноисса, тетка Раймонды	Г-жа Чеветта.
Бѣлая дама, покровительница дома Дорисъ	Г-жа Сиверская.
Клеманисъ подруги Раймонды	Г-жа Куличевская.
Генріетта	Г-жа Преображенская.
Рыцарь Жанъ де-Бріенъ, женихъ Раймонды	Г-нъ Легатъ 3-й.
Андрей II, король венгерскій	Г-нъ Аистовъ.
Абдеррахманъ, сарацинскій рыцарь	Г-нъ Гердтъ.
Бернаръ де-Вантадуръ, провансальскій трубадуръ	Г-нъ Кякштъ.
Беранже, аквитанскій трубадуръ	Г-нъ Легатъ 1-й.
Сенешаль, управляющій замкомъ Дорисъ	Г-нъ Булгаковъ.
Кавалеръ изъ свиты де-Бріенъ	Г-нъ Солянниковъ 2.
Венгерскій рыцарь	Г-нъ Гиллертъ.
	Г-нъ Татариновъ.
Сарацинскіе рыцари	Г-нъ Воронинъ.
	Г-нъ Бальцеръ.
	Г-нъ Быковъ.

Дамы, вассалы, рыцари венгерскіе, сарацинскіе, герольды, мавры, провансальцы, королевскіе солдаты и слуги

A Russian poster announcing the first performance of *Raymonda.*

Chapter II
The History of Raymonda. *The Libretto of the Ballet*

It is common knowledge that ballet music was beginning to earn recognition as a serious genre in the 19th century. P. Tchaikovsky was the first to achieve this in Russian art. His three ballets, *Swan Lake, The Sleeping Beauty, The Nutcracker* introduced a new level in ballet scores. The reformer himself explained the essence of the reformism; Tchaikovsky said: "Ballet is a kind of symphony itself." It stirred the minds of composers but nevertheless ballet was traditionally considered a minor genre.

Glazunov worshiped Tchaikovsky's talent, admired his ballets, but was not impatient to begin writing ballet scores. The idea of *Raymonda* doesn't belong to him. Coincidence gave birth to this masterpiece by Glazunov.

In 1895, Ivan Vsevolozhsky, director of the Imperial Theatres of Russia received a scenario of *Raymonda* from Y. Pashkova, a writer and journalist who wrote sometimes in Russian and sometimes in French. Her works were not brilliant; they were entertaining.

But the Mariinsky Theater in Petersburg had already cooperated with her. She wrote a scenario of the ballet *Cinderella* which was staged there in 1893. It was a success primarily thanks to Petipa who by that time had brilliantly headed the ballet in Petersburg for 50 years and won worldwide fame.

Hence the wish of the script writer to continue the cooperation. This time she offered not a fairy tale but a real topic from the Middle Ages. She wrote it on the basis of legends and historical novels.

The action of the ballet takes place in the epoch of the crusades. In a medieval castle a birthday party is being given for young Raymonda, a niece of Countess de Doris. The guests are enjoying the music, dancing, fencing. The countess points to a statue of a woman in the garden saying that she is a White Lady, a ghost, a protectress of the house and family of de Doris. Raymonda is happily excited; her fiancé, Hungarian knight Jean de Brien, is to return from a crusade the next day. In the twilight Raymonda falls asleep and has a prophetic dream; the White Lady comes to life and takes her to a magic garden where she sees her fiancé. She rushes to him with joy but suddenly there appears an Oriental sheik in his place. Raymonda wakes up in horror.

The second act starts with everyone in the castle getting ready to meet the fiancé. Noble guests are coming to the castle. There comes Saracen sheik Abderakhman with his entourage. Raymonda is horrified; she recognizes the "hero" of her dream. Abderakhman falls passionately in love with her and constantly follows her everywhere. He tries to lure her with expensive gifts, but Raymonda refuses all his claims with indignation.

Abderakhman orders his retinue to dance for her. When the dances are in full swing Adkerakhman tries to abduct Raymonda. At this very moment Jean de Brien appears and with the protection of the White Lady kills the sheik in a duel. The third act shows the wedding party. Hungarian King Andrey II who was with de Brien in the crusade is present at the wedding party as an honored guest.

The plot is simple but the weakest point is its dramatic composition. The first act lacks any action. The heroes of the ballet are static. Raymonda is always in her dreams, sometimes in reality and sometimes while asleep. Both male heroes come onto stage only in the second act and the main one, de Brien, appears at the very end of the act; he is absent for more than a half of the play.

There were many moments in the scenario which couldn't be expressed with the help of the dance. For example the Countess's "story" about the White Lady or the reading of the letter that a herald brings, announcing de Brien's arrival.

However Vsevolozhsky regarded Pashkova's work with favor. He was attracted by the theme of a noble devoted love, the refined background of the action and its exotic contrasts. He wanted a play magnificently rich in colors. A man of good education and refinement, Vsevolozhsky certainly saw the drawbacks of the scenario. Besides it must be remembered that Vsevolozhsky himself wrote the scenario of such a first-class ballet as *The Sleeping Beauty*. And now before showing the new scenario to Petipa the director had edited it. The famous choreographer made his corrections, but he also agreed to stage the ballet after he had read it for the first time.

So the fate of the scenario was decided. The only problem left was a composer. All agreed that Glazunov was the right one.

Chapter III
The Music of Raymonda

By the time the scenario of *Raymonda* was written Glazunov was a famous composer in the prime of his creative life. The director and the choreographer wanted to continue the cooperation with great composers; they remembered their invaluable experience of work with Tchaikovsky.

There was one more circumstance that also pushed them to choosing Glazunov among other great Russian composers.

Glazunov's *Coronation Cantata* for solo voices, chorus and orchestra commissioned by the Imperial Ministry was performed at a ceremonial dinner at the Hall of Facets in the presence of the royal family, high officials and foreign guests on May 14, 1896. The emperor liked it. One of Glazunov's waltzes was performed by the emperor's orchestra at another ceremonial party nine days later. Vsevolozhsky wrote about this waltz with admiration in his letter to Petipa: "It's a good combination of Delibes with Tchaikovsky. Sure, this man was born to compose ballets for us."

And he was right. Glazunov's turn to ballet was the realization of tendencies which always existed in his creative work.

One can find many dances among little pieces written by the composer in his childhood and youth. Later there appeared quite a few of them too. For example in the '90's Glazunov's concerto waltzes (for symphony orchestra) were written and rapidly became famous. The first of them—very noble, refined with a flexible, expressive melody—became particularly popular.

Besides dances themselves there are many compositions by Glazunov which are of some "dancing character." A special plasticity of melodies, richness, variety of rhythms are characteristic of many works by the composer.

There is a suite among symphonic works by young Glazunov which includes such danceable themes as: *Tarantella, Oriental Dance, Cracovienne, Lezghinka* and a *Suite Caracteristique* containing a *Village Dance, Oriental Dance, March, Mazurka, Wedding Dance* and others.

Later Glazunov orchestrated a number of Chopin's works and created *Chopiniana*, a suite on Chopin's themes which served as a basis of M. Fokine's ballet *Les Sylphides*. After that he wrote *Ballet Suite*, a number of orchestral dances and marches.

Hence we can say the composer was approaching ballet almost from the very beginning. No wonder that having been commissioned for *Raymonda* he was glad to start working at it.

The influence of Tchaikovsky, who lived in Moscow, which we have already mentioned was another reason too. In addition, they were personally acquainted, met many times and wrote to each other.

Their interest was mutual. Tchaikovsky was impressed with Glazunov's talent when the latter was very young. When Glazunov's *First Symphony* was performed in Moscow for the first time, Tchaikovsky in his letter to Petersburg asked the famous composer Balakirev about him.

Glazunov wrote: "Later I came to know Peter Ilyich better. Then we became good friends and our friendship lasted until his death." "I appreciate your talent very much"—Tchaikovsky wrote to Glazunov in 1890.

On October 16, 1893 Glazunov was present at the première of the *Sixth Symphony* by Tchaikovsky who conducted it. They returned from the concert together. On the 25th of October Tchaikovsky died.

Beginning the work on *Raymonda* Glazunov felt he was a successor to his great older friend. He strived for the same unity of music and drama composition in the ballet when the music does not merely accompany dances, but creates images, heroes, characters, their relations in a complex combination of feelings, moods, passions . . .

Glinka's music was an example of an earlier period. Glazunov admitted: "I consider dances of the third act of *Ruslan* the crown of ballet style." The plot of the offered ballet was interesting and appealed to the composer. Glazunov easily transferred his imagination to the romantic epoch of the Middle Ages to which he had been attracted since his childhood. He read many books about those times, knew the historic events very well, was aware of the peculiarities of everyday life of the past. The Middle Ages were not for him merely a page or chapter from a textbook or a list of facts but a real, vivid, interesting epoch with its own essential quality which he felt. Glazunov spoke with enthusiasm about knighthood and knights, about poet-singers (troubadours), trouveres and minstrels, about performances on the squares of medieval towns and about life in castles. B. V. Asafiev wrote: "These stories inspired by the imagination of a most talented Russian musician convinced and gave birth to admiration."

Not long before Glazunov started working at *Raymonda* he had been deeply impressed by historical monuments. He travelled through Germany in 1895. The blackened remnants of knights' castles, the massive walls of cathedrals—all these witnesses of crusades impressed him. "Lately I've been under the impression of the medieval monuments"—he wrote to Stasov from Nuremberg on September 16. A bit earlier, at the end of August he picturesquely described to Rimsky-Korsakov a famous monument of medieval architecture—the Cologne Cathedral: "I thought while looking intensely at all the details of the construction there was some movement in its 'Motionless sounds'—it's like some architectural poem . . ."

The East, particularly its music, was of interest to Glazunov. Both this element and a Spanish one (which was of no less interest to the composer) were to play an important part in *Raymonda*.

Thus a chance to work at *Raymonda* was very attractive to Glazunov. Now he was eager to begin. Three days after he had finished his *Sixth Symphony* he started working at the ballet. He wrote the first episodes of *Raymonda* on August 16, 1896. He wrote them when he was still involved with his symphony and the sounds of *Raymonda* combined with the sounds of the symphony explain the noble origin of Glazunov's ballet firstling. The work went rapidly. It took a year and a half for the ballet to be finished and ready for staging.

Though the plot can be easily retold in a few words, the ballet by Glazunov is a large composition of three acts. Here we see the composer armed with his experience and talent, generously presenting listeners with wonderful music. It is not by chance that the ballet has been kept in the repertoires of theatres even now and its fragments are often performed at concerts.

Following Tchaikovsky's style Glazunov also symphonizes the ballet. The logic and harmony of musical development, expressiveness, full-blooded images are very attractive in the composition.

A number of the best scenes are devoted to the heroine of the ballet. Not only joyful feelings of a youthful, carefree fiancée are connected with her but a much richer range of emotions, from enthusiastic love to dramatic despair.

The grand adagio of the first act belongs to the scenes of the former type (in a dream Raymonda meets her fiancé). It is based on a lyrical melody typical of Glazunov. Performed by a solo violin it flows widely and passionately, full of joy and light and is regarded a song of a happy life.

Raymonda's conflicts with Abderakhman are in contrast to such lyrical duets. The music here is filled with the alarm, trouble, despair which seized the heroine.

However, in Glazunov's ballets, the same as in his compositions of other genres, the lyrico-epic principle prevails.

Raymonda is often called a monumental ballet and this is justified. Dancing images, mass scenes (there are many of them in the ballet) make such an impression. These dancing suites of a kind characterize the background surrounding the main heroes (first of all Raymonda herself).

Mass scenes in the ballet are various. They are the best proof of the boundless inventiveness of the composer. All three acts of the ballet are full of dances which have their own particular features.

The dances of Abderakhman's entourage (act II) are of great importance. Jugglers, Arabian boys, Saracens, Spaniards all march one by one before Raymonda, who is worried by the appearance of the Saracen whom she had dreamed about. Their performance is very colorful, full of temperament and makes a vivid Spanish-Arabian suite. Passionate and full of fire, the sometimes wild dances of Abderakhman's servants indirectly characterize him too. They are in great contrast to Raymonda and they underline a deep difference between them. But that's not all. Dances of Abderakhman's company follow in such order that the dynamics of the development continuously grow. They acquire more temperament, become more rapid, turn into a general bacchanalia and with this both Raymonda's worry and a tense expectation of the audience grow. The tension of dynamics prepares the culmination of this scene: Abderakhman tries to abduct Raymonda but Jean de Brien prevents him from doing it.

Thus a number of dances are included into a general development of music which logically goes to the acme and then to the denouément—the duel in which the fiancé wins. The Spanish-Arabian suite of the second act is a vivid example of a developed mass scene with a unity of music and inner integrity.

The Spanish dance is the "pearl" of the suite. The composer created the musical image with the help of laconic means and simple ways but he did it very precisely. This image seems to have ideally focused our ideas of original dances of Spaniards—passionate dances to the accompaniment of a guitar and castanets. That's why this part is so unusually popular, why it's constantly performed as a separate choreographic item.

A chain of dances with a certain national coloring is included into the third act of the ballet. Among them there is a Hungarian suite (de Brien is a Hungarian knight). Glazunov learned the typical features of Hungarian music and used them wonderfully in his dances. The grand Hungarian dance which resembles a ceremonial march is one of the most popular dances of the suite. It is usually performed by a symphony orchestra as a separate piece.

Of course, such deep penetration into the nature of music of different nationalities was possible due to a constant, attentive interest in it. All his life the composer kept the interest in folklore he showed early in his youth. During his trips Glazunov would listen to performers of different nationalities: Spaniards, Italians, Hungarians, the French . . .

In contrast with Abderakhman and de Brien, Raymonda and her surroundings are described by a transparent, gentle, airy music. In the first act among numerous dances of this kind the grand Waltz stands out as one of the most lyrical episodes of the ballet. The beauty and nobleness of the music, a singing, plastic melody, a lyricism expressed in it made the waltz very popular. The scene of Raymonda's dreams is full of romantic excited passion.

However, every scene has its unique merits. *Raymonda* is one of the greatest peaks of Glazunov's works. After *Raymonda* he wrote two more one-act ballets, *Ruses d'amour* and *The Seasons*. The former is a graceful pastorale in the spirit of French art of the 18th century about love intrigues; the latter is a plotless, allegoric ballet.

Left to right: Ilya Ginzburg, Vladimir Stasov, Feodor Chaliapin and Alexander Glazunov.

Maya Plisetskaya as Raymonda and Alexander Rudenko as de Brienne. Below: Another older production of *Raymonda* with Marina Semyonova as Raymonda.

Chapter IV

Versions of Raymonda

Thanks to Glazunov's music and Petipa's choreography *Raymonda* became a ballet of classical heritage of the world ballet theatre. But since its first performance in the Mariinsky Theatre it has undergone several versions, due mainly to the weak scenario by Y. Pashkova. It was the scenario that was improved and completed in the first place. It met the requirements of the beginning of the century when the ballet art aimed at "life like reality" and became more necessary in the 30's—40's when the ballet based on the drama developed its staging and literary basis. The plot of *Raymonda* was being defined concretely, it was being rid of pantomimic absurdity and incomprehensible stagings. The versions by A. Gorsky (1908), L. Lavrovsky (1945), K. Sergeev (1948) won recognition. The authors of the new versions wanted to decipher "unintelligible" parts of the scenario. Thus they wished to emphasize that it was Raymonda's fiancé who visited her in her dream. For this purpose some choreographers put de Brien's portrait in the first scene, others, the tapestry with his portrait. These came to life in the scene of the "dream."

It undoubtedly did improve the scenario but did not relieve the play from inertness as the other hero, sheik Abderakhman, was very passive though he appears long before de Brien. He came to propose to de Brien's fiancé in de Brien's absence. Naturally Raymonda immediately turned Abderakhman down. And though he remained on the stage for the whole act, while his splendid company displayed itself in dances, it did not change the situation. Abderakhman did not act. According to classical canons a negative hero could express himself only by pantomime. Despite all their efforts the actors just did not have enough material for the complex personification of this hero. Abderakhman's attempt to abduct Raymonda makes the denouement of the second act a bit livelier. But the fiancé came in time and won the duel and thus let the audience and his financée finally have a good look at him at the wedding part in the third act.

In fact once in V. Vainonen's version in 1938 an attempt was made to give the two heroes an active life. Then they were included into action from the very beginning of the ballet. The whole scenario was completely changed. The heroes even changed their lines of character. De Brien became insidious and Abderakhman, who turned into his captive—positive. Raymonda gave her love to the latter. A new entertaining and well-composed plot was undoubtedly interesting. But the classical *Raymonda* in which whole acts changed places was ruined. Alien though witty ideas, "supports" from the outside never benefit a ballet, an opera or a play. The version of 1938 eloquently proved once more: "the insignificant plot" is strangely linked (with indissoluble ties) with the outstanding music and choreography of *Raymonda* and steadily resists any alteration.

We may now ask if it is possible at all to write a new plot for a ballet which has a classical recognized original? And are we at a deadlock with obstinate *Raymonda*? Its new version in the Bolshoi Theatre proves we are not.

G. Kirilova as Raymonda and R. Gerber as Abderakhman in the Leningrad Kirov Theater production.

26

Chapter V

The Play by Marius Petipa

As it had been with *The Sleeping Beauty*, Petipa started to work at *Raymonda* before the composer finished it. Moreover (and this was also the experience of *The Sleeping Beauty*) he dictated his conditions to the composer: rhythms, tempos, type of music, activity of the episodes and scenes. And as was Tchaikovsky in his time, Glazunov was not against it. According to his own words, these "letters" were convenient to him. The "letters" freed him from many formal things, gave him time for inspired creation of the lyrical sense of the images. Glazunov used to praise Petipa orally and proved the sincerity of his praises by devoting the score of *Raymonda* to the company of the Mariinsky Theater taught by Petipa.

The choreographer drew up orders and plans for the composer and at their fulfillment realized them in choreographic images at the rehearsal halls. The work was progressing rapidly. Glazunov often attended the rehearsals sometimes substituting for the leader of the orchestra.

While staging the play Petipa continued working at the scenario wishing to make it more impressive. He worked with great enthusiasm, perhaps realizing his role in the creation of the masterpiece which would belong to history. Though he changed some details of the scenario, he was, like Glazunov (who did not interfere with the work of the scenario writer) busy with his own art-choreography. It was choreography that he used to elevate the plot, to enlarge the conflict, to express deeper and more delicately the natures of the heroes.

For instance, the choreographer invented a great Pas d'action for the second act. Together with two pairs of friends, Raymonda and Abderakhman take part in it. True, following the canons of his theatre Petipa did not give the sheik a dancing "language." But his participation here made it possible to show in vivid movements a passionate love for Raymonda who in her gala dance introduced her house, family, her company to the guest.

The history of the ballet

I 1900-1908
Conductor – A. Arends
Choreographers – I. Khlustin, A. Gorsky
Designers – K. Valtz, P. Isakov

II 1908-1915
Conductor – A. Arends
Choreographer – A. Gorsky
Designer – K. Korovin

III 1918-1939
Conductor – Ju. Fayer
Choreographer – A. Gorsky
Designer – K. Korovin

IV April 7, 1949
Conductor – Yu. Fayer
Choreographer – A. Gorsky, staged in version
of L. Lavrovsky
Designer – S. Kobuladze

V June 29, 1984
Conductor – A. Ziuraitis
Choreographer – M. Petipa, revised version
by Yu. Grigorovich
Designer – S. Virsaldaze

A.K. GLAZUNOV (1865-1936).

Conductor
Algis Ziuraitis

Choreographer
Yuri Grigorovich

Designer
Simon Virsaladze

RAYMONDA

Natalya Bessmertnova   Lyudmila Semenyaka

JEAN DE BRIENNE

Irek Mukhammedov   Alexander Bogatyrev

ABDERAKHMAN

Gediminas Taranda   Yuri Vetrov

The choreographer and the composer shared the idea that the play must be based on striking contrasts. The choreography of *Raymonda* is big ensembles-suites during the whole ballet. The suites are now classical dances—on the tips of the toes, in tutus; now character dances—on the heels, picturesque and colorful with much energy and temperament. Thus did Petipa realize dramatic composition in choreography. Unlike the dramatic content of the scenario, the choreographic one was impressive. It gave the action tension, acuity, dynamism. Thus Petipa's genius could produce unexpected effects despite a weak scenario.

Classical dance contrasted with a character dance exposes the everlasting struggle of elevated life and earthly life. This very important moment was particularly underlined by Y. Grigorovich in his new version of *Raymonda*.

Petipa constructing the ballet like an experienced architect, considered the chief idea that of woman's alluring beauty, attracting different souls by its purity, and nobleness, obeying only its own supreme laws.

In his creative work Petipa is a poet of femininity, a knight of the ballerina. He puts woman in the center of "the universe" in all his ballets, makes all admire her, worship her. *Raymonda* in this respect was just ideal for him.

His *Raymonda* is a ballet-portrait of the heroine who reigns throughout the play. There is not another play in the history of ballet in which a heroine has so many dances and each one so different. *Raymonda* gives the heroine the opportunity to show all the sides of her talent, all the colors of a classical dance. It is a rococo dance, rapid and frisky in the first scene of the first act. It is a romantic timid, impressionistic mysterious dance in the second scene—a dream in the same act. It is sculpturally expressive and contains the strictness of classicism in the second act. And in the third act Petipa staged a spicy refined character dance.

The choreographer started the third act with a mazurka, a Hungarian dance—for adults and children (the fiancé and the king are Hungarians). For the fiancé and the fiancée he staged something unprecedented—a Classical Hungarian Grand pas. Here some elements of Hungarian dances were put into the positions of arms, bodies in classical pas and they became wonderfully refined and exotically beautiful. This grand pas is the best of masterpieces even for Petipa. However the whole of *Raymonda* consists of masterpieces of one kind or another. History has already proved that it is a culmination of the genius of Petipa. *Raymonda* lives on victoriously in the world of ballet theatres.

But we must remember that every epoch chooses its own esthetics. Ballet was primarily a feminine art in the 19th century . . . A man had the right to be a partner, a tactful, careful cavalier who helped a heroine make a brilliant display—meanwhile nobly remaining in the shadow. The main positive hero did not have his own dances; he danced only one variation in the denouément in pas de deux which was usually gala, ceremonial. And a negative character's part was all pantomimic. It seems paradoxical today but according to the etiquette it was improper for people of high rank to jump and roll. And in all plays princes, counts, sheiks were in the center . . . But the right for a dance belonged to people of lower rank.

Petipa belonged to his age and followed its traditions. He constructed the parts of de Brien and Abderakhman according to the canons customary at that time. However in *Raymonda* he staged many fine male dances, in the main, all character dances. In the second act it is the whole suite-oriental which includes dances: Saracen, dance of Arabian boys, Moorish and finally Spanish inadvertently underlining the Spanish-Moorish contents of that epoch. The male and female dancers can equally display themselves here, the same as in the third act, in the Hungarian dance and the mazurka. Petipa gave a brilliant example of a male classical dance too—a dance of four youths in the classical Hungarian Grand pas. It is kind of a tournament of young troubadours who compete in adroitness, strength, courage. It is mastery of a very complex dance; usually only the most talented soloists take part in it.

The première of *Raymonda* took place on the 7th of January, 1898, conducted by R. Drigo, the best conductor of that time. The main parts were: Raymonda: Piarina Jeniana (an Italian ballerina who worked in Russia); Jean de Brien: Sergei Legat (a representative of a Russian ballet dynasty); Abderakhman: Paul Gerdt (an outstanding dancer of the Mariinsky Theatre whose nobleness of style was unsurpassed). The scenery and costumes were made by O. Allegri, K. Ivanov, L. Lambin.

The play was a great success and welcomed unanimously. Since that time it has been performed on the stages of many Russian theatres. It is equally famous abroad too.

The troupe paying tribute to Petipa and Glazunov at opening night.

Yuri Grigorovich was coaxed into wearing his medals for this historic photograph.

_____ Chapter VI _____
The Play of Yuri Grigorovich

Yuri Grigorovich, the author of the new version chooses a qualitatively new approach different from that of his predecessors. He studies the main "text" of the ballet as the music and choreography are much deeper than the plot. The plot here is just a support, it only sets up landmarks, like a program in program symphonic compositions. This is a modern opinion of a ballet. But as we see, Petipa shared it. He accepted cumbersome scenarios of his time but did not become their captive; he developed them on the basis of his own choreographic conception and enriched a dramatic composition of the scenario by his dramatic composition of images.

Having given a new life to classical *Raymonda* on the stage Grigorovich did not ruin the scenario of it.

He created a great volume of new choreographic material. The sketches of both heroes turned into images with their own dances. Jean de Brien alone who did not have his own dances before and was just a partner of the ballerina, now has six new items. Meanwhile this innovation exists in absolute unity with the old choreography.

So de Brien immediately appears on the stage now and for the first time in the history of *Raymonda* participates in the whole of the first scene. While he has always been present here from the very beginning, but it was in the music which, starting with the introduction de Brien's theme, interlaces with that of the heroine. His theme is presented by fanfares and choral music in the first act. Before that this music accompanied various pantomimic episodes in which heralds, vassals, and pages acted, at the same time introducing de Brien. Grigorovich includes de Brien into the action preserving the old scenic contours but enriching them from inside.

There has always been the Grand Waltz with Raymonda taking part in it in the first act. In the new version de Brien participates in it. The ballerina heroine is given a partner—a sweetheart, surrounding them, the troubadours and their girl friends and a chief troubadour. There is an event in the scene that was a variety entertainment before; the two lovers meet and their love is told in the waltz, animating its imaginative beauty. Raymonda and her fiancé are not just one more couple. A pas de deux by the lovers blossoms out of the flower bud within the waltz—an adagio; the same happens to the male variation, a coda created by Grigorovich, the famous female variation of pizzicato which has always been here. Thus the heroes "tell" about themselves and their love for each other. This is the dawn of their love quietly happy, full of joy.

The dances substitute for pantomimic episodes. The knight's dance of de Brien surrounded by his armor-bearers replaces the long entrances of vassals and heralds. The severe world of battles is suddenly recalled, disturbing the gentle harmony of pure lyricism, displaying a different type of beauty—that of noble manhood, turning the inspired knight, poet of the wonderful lady into a warrior, her brave defender.

In some cases the new choreography provides continuation to the old scenes. The music which has not displayed itself on the stage now does. The music of intervals is used for duets which now finalize both the first scene (the lovers' parting) and the second act (their meeting after de Brien's crusade). The image of de Brien is being developed during the whole play. By the classical canons it is the image of an ideal hero. But by the modern canons de Brien's image is not static; it is a many-sided character full of vitality. He also displays himself in the poetic madrigal of the Grand Waltz and in the pathetic knight's dance, in the love duets and variations of a different nature. In Grigorovich's interpretation—de Brien is a symbolic and complex image. He is a personification of an elevated, poetic, harmonious world.

A. Bogatirev, the first dancer of de Brien's role, deeply penetrated into this wholehearted part and it was probably his best work. The dancer himself with his aristocratic dancing manners was very good for the part. His extraordinary graceful movements are the main thing. They show the admiration of the knight-poet who worships woman's beauty. To her glory are his crusades, to her honor are his duels. A. Bogatirev's de Brien is an illuminated image combining courage, tenderness and nobleness. De Brien's dancing part created by Grigorovich told anew on the heroine's part. It has been enriched by new motives.

In the first scene after a splendid day dusk fell and Raymonda continued dreaming of her fiancé in the famous variation with a veil. In Petipa's play the veil is just a detail of her dress. In Grigorovich's version the veil is presented by the fiancé at the moment of their parting. This changed the essence of the variation. It looks like a reflection of the heroine's impressions of the day, like reminiscences of her happy moments, but now they are full of light sadness. The game with the veil became a recollection of the gentle touches of the lover In solitude Raymonda's feelings and thoughts emphasized by her real meeting with de Brien become sharper. They continue in her dreams and her heart is full of new wishes. This is a psychological basis for another scene of the dream. It is a dream-garden where the White Lady takes Raymonda. The White Lady was not always lucky in other versions: they occasionally excluded her. But now as in Petipa's play there is a statue of the White Lady in the first scene which comes to life in the second scene.

As an image of the knight's poetry, a symbol of fate, the White Lady is preserved in the version by Grigorovich. It maintains the style and spirit of this classical play, its ancient lyricism and shows in the present context its metaphorical many-sided nature. In her white glimmering dress, majestically dominating on the tips of the toes, she is the center of all this mysteriously-shadowed stage. She is a symbol of the heroine's soul, a support for her activity, purity in the vortex of confused feelings, luring expectations, frightening forebodings.

In the scene of dreams we can see Petipa's choreography in which Grigorovich revived very important things lost in the previous versions. It concerns a corps-de-ballet which light accompaniment now seems to echo gentle sighs of the heroes' adagio. It concerns the two women soloists, the six female leading figures; today their participation in the dances has substantially increased, particularly in the denouement. The revived details like an artful restoration enlivened the picture and "supported" its psychological implication. The estranged romantic beauty found a new life. And the garden of dreams is the innermost recesses of a mysterious woman's soul. Every moment of a great dancing composition (not only the heroine's dances) is a personification of the confusing feelings of waking up in love. The girlish dreams are found here in careful "flies about" of the corps-de-ballet. The trembling of the heart agitated by the expectation is symbolized by the "twittering" of wheeling around round dances. The sorrow of love is in the sweet bliss of solo variations. The passions are in the anxious flights.

Grigorovich "found" a deep meaning of this melancholy and abstract scene of the dream where he saw the life of the heart which was now thirsty for love.

In Petipa's variant Abderakhman appeared in the first scene preceding the scene of the dream. The choreographer persuaded Glazunov to compose the music for the Saracen's entrance in addition to the score which had already been written.

Grigorovich did without the Saracen's entrance in the first scene in accordance with the composer's intention. He also freed Abderakhman from the features of a villain and this was in accordance with the music which pictures the Saracen and his surrounding in a complex way: not as negative, but as a different world, attractive in its own way too but contrasting and alien to the Romantic palace of Raymonda. He equipped Abderakhman with his dancing language according to the same principle as with de Brien. His pantomimic episodes are substituted by dancing ones now. In addition he is included into the dances of the character suite where before he was only present in them.

He appears in the second act as a guest and sees Raymonda for the first time. And if the second scene of the first act is called the dream of Raymonda, we can now name the second act the dream of Abderakhman eager to achieve the impossible. The dreams of the heroine come true. She gets to know a strange world—alien but attractive, alluring . . .

At the same time the second act is a temptation of the woman's soul, a test of her faithfulness.

Today Abderakhman lures, tempts and is being lured himself; he is possessed by a destructive, pernicious dream he can't live without. G. Taranda shows it brilliantly and powerfully on a very high tragic level. His hero passionate and obsessed by love throws at the feet of his love his power, might, position—with no thought for his dignity—ready to make any sacrifice to his love.

There is such a rival of "the white" knight in the new version by Grigorovich that Raymonda can't just refuse him angrily and with repugnance. She fears his uncontrolled impulse but she is attracted by his earthly passion; she is agitated by the freedom of feelings which disdained the norms of etiquette. This Raymonda makes her choice having passed the test of the seduction.

Now a complex psychological "symphony" devoted to the relations of the heroine and her guest is being elaborated starting with Pas d'action which opens the second act and more precisely with the sextet of Raymonda, her two girl-friends, their partners and Abderakhman. Grigorovich delicately created an image of concord in the first scene of the ballet which told about the happy love: he gave it the form of a duet dance (the duet as a choreographic symbol of mutual love). Raymonda and de Brien are together all the time. It is different with Abderakhman. He never has a real duet with Raymonda, but there continuously appear intriguing moments in the choreography, twin movements of different kinds and yet which come apart again. The irresponsible love and as its dance sign indicates a yearning for the duet, its inaccessibility are the leit-motif of the second act . . . Pas d'action, ceremonial and regal before, in which the uninvited claimant had been tolerated only due to prevailing etiquette was turned by Grigorovich into an excited and tense meeting of two different souls from different worlds: the Oriental sheik seeks the French countess's love despite their curiosity and distrust of each other. A whimsical pattern of the continuously changing couples of the sextet, in which Abderakhman is very active now, is filled with aching anxiety. The heroes exist here in a kind of distrustful attraction and repulsion and Raymonda is an ideal mysteriously stealing away and luring by its illusive closeness, an unexpressed promise of the duet.

The Oriental suite following him shows the splendid court of the Saracen and now it also exposes the world of his internal feelings, ideas of a happy love. On the height of his feelings for the first time in the history of *Raymonda* he joins "Panaderos," a Spanish dance. Grigorovich in his own way wonderfully found a place for Abderakhman in this very dance as if connecting western and eastern cultures solved the problem of their difference and interinfluence. There is a contination of the theme of the yearning for the duet in *Panaderos* which has been composed anew by Grigorovich. There are two women soloists instead of the leading pair (as in Petipa's version) and lonely Abderakhman is in the center. "Panaderos" is his passionate confession, ecstasy and despair of love, his seduction of Raymonda and supplications to her.

Like a mysterious answer to this burst of feelings there appears the Oriental dance which today, as in the unrealized plans of Petipa is given to Raymonda. Abderakhman reverentially following her joins the intriguing dance-invocation full of sad and trying sweet bliss. It excites by a new illusion of the duet. And as if provoked by this the bacchanalia starts with the earthly, sensual, carnal world exposing vividness of vitality, an impudent brilliance of the wild element, the beauty of fearless passions and feelings. Grigorovich doesn't stress the episode of Raymonda's abduction, making it metaphorical. Suddenly the heroine is high above all in Abderakhman's hands. In this way an original flexible accent is created—a pause in the middle of the continuing bacchanal dance. A certain shining image inaccessible in its purity rises as if above a seething sea. The appearance of the "white knight" de Brien is understood as a choice of the heroine to help her dispel her confused feelings. And the duel which Grigorovich made in a very spectacular dancing form is a reflection of the emotional struggle of Raymonda who has resisted the temptation and of Abderakhman who having not won in his love seeks a defeat-death in life. However the duel is really terrible. The duel is a defense of its dignity and beauty by each of the two clashed worlds. And the duet of Raymonda and de Brien after the battle scene completes the second act: the return of rest after the terrible storms, the triumph of fidelity after hard trials, peace of soul with the wisdom of life. The two duets made up by Grigorovich, *The Farewell* (the first scene) and *The Meeting* (the denouement of the second act) are represented in the play as peculiar landmarks. The whole of life is full of dangers, temptations, confusions. In *The Farewell* the heroes enter a new world leaving at home their careless happiness and the tranquillity which accompanies innocence. But they meet, having realized their love and attitude to their life. And then comes the third act—"The Wedding Party." In the new version it is almost "unchanged." Everything belongs to Petipa. How wonderfully did Grigorovich make us see a new internal sense of the "old" choreography.

He interprets the third act as happy fulfillment—a wished-for harmony and love. Created by Petipa, the classical Hungarian Grand pas in which character elements penetrate into the classical dance enriching and decorating it becomes the culmination of this in accordance with the whole content. There is not only proud triumph in it but also warmth, cordiality, lyricism; there is life in it, life which has been realized through suffering. The new variation of de Brien becomes a symbol of the earthly triumph. It is made with the music of a children's Hungarian dance in which touching infantilism is absent, but impulse, frankness, freedom are present. And the delicate variation of Raymonda is presented as meditations of the past. It seems paradoxical but having enlarged the men's portraits Grigorovich enlarged Petipa's very idea of *Raymonda* a female ballet. And the difference of *Raymonda* from *The Sleeping Beauty* (they were often called twins) is particularly evident now. *The Sleeping Beauty* is about girlhood, about first love. *Raymonda* is about a flourishing femininity, about a woman's love seeking for harmony, about a mysterious soul which preserves its whole heartedness in spite of its inconsistencies.

Thanks go to N. Bessmertnova whose art showed us the depth and subtlety of the new version of *Raymonda*. Bessmertnova dances in this most difficult ballet after she had danced in a series of premières of modern plays. She is the most elegant classical ballerina whose mystery is not only in a canonical strictness but also in a lively beauty of the academic school. We see her as a very modern artist capable of returning the charm of the new to the classics. Her dance has a rare combination of airiness, a transparent and refined sensuality; she creates an image aristocratic in spirit and passionate in heart. Her Raymonda is a whole philosophy of woman's nature in which fidelity and self-will, tenderness and obstinacy, fearlessness and unprotectedness, steadfastness and fragility fascinatingly coexist . . . Bessmertnova leads her heroine through troubles to the greatness of love.

Glazunov's score, the source of the new choreographic interpretation, was renewed by conductor A. Zhuraitis and his orchestra. The music in which an epic tranquility, a triumphal brilliance were mainly valued, is today full of many emotional nuances. The music and the action are so interwoven that they do not seem to be able to exist separately, but immediately turn into dance. And this animated dance music is also enriched by picturesque color and light.

S. Versaladze has designed the scenery and costumes in *Raymonda* many times. His inexhaustible imagination impresses us. Versaladze's scenes are in their own way "laconic," only a fragment of a medieval castle, the front door to the palace, decorated with light steps of the staircase. There is a ballet elegance in the scenery. There are no heavy textures here, the entrance to the palace is made of a picturesque tulle back drop combining silver and gold on the white background. And at the same time a majestic Gothic spirit reigns in a strict beauty of proportions in a tracery, its rise to the skies light and proud lines. The art of the scenery, costumes and light is in the most delicate counterpoint. Thus the ceremonial dresses of the courtiers become a live architectural element as if putting the last touches to the contours of the castle. And in the dresses of the "dreams" that whimsical foliage which trails over the staircase mysteriously flickering in the moonlight seems to come to life.

A real leit-motif development of a refined palette of colors in which the colors express the feelings of the play takes place during the whole ballet. In the first scene, when the serene heroine is on the threshold of her life, her spring tutu is pale blue. In the second act, when the temptations and seductions are in store for her, she is white as a symbol of purity and steadfastness. And at last, in the third act her tutu is turquoise. A saturated, full-blooded color for Raymonda with her life experience now seems to have been born by the condensation of the previous pale blue color. All work of Versaladze has a deep internal sense. Clear, transparent, spring water-colors and the light of the first scene repeat the pure feelings of the heroes. The image of the Oriental suite is in contrast with this. There are shades of metal here: silver-steel, bronze, brownish-black, given as if through a haze as a reflection of Abderakhman's unachievable dreams. And suddenly his wild hopes return and the same happens to the colors—a daring touch, an impudent collision: a flash of bright crimson in the women's dresses of *Panaderos*, a piercingly blue southern sky in the dresses of the Saracen dancers . . . And in this picturesque "symphony" the color white has its own special "tune": at the beginning it is dazzlingly white—in the costume of de Brien, then as if being frightened by its own splendor it turns to anxious glimmering in the dresses of the White Lady: and then it becomes calm, appeasing—in the tutu of Raymonda. Versaladze's colors "undergo" trials together with the heroes of the ballet. They are so strikingly bound up with the dances that if you stop the action at any time you'll see a perfect—in its composition—picture.

This play which has become an event in the life of ballet art is notable for a rare harmony of music, dance and painting. Galina Ulanova said about it: "The new *Raymonda* is an example of what a classical play should be today."

Synopsis of the Grigorovich Production

There is a birthday party at the Palace of the French Countess Sibil de Doris. The party is honoring her niece, Raymonda, who is showered with attention from her guests and her fiancé. Jean de Brienne, the fiancé of Raymonda, must leave the party early, for he is a Crusader and must leave for the war under the command of Andrey II, King of Hungary. Thus the birthday party is also a farewell party.

Countess Sibil tells the bride-to-be about a beautiful white statue in her garden. This statue comes to life at night as a ghost. But there is nothing to fear, for this ghost, the White Lady, is the protectoress of the Palace and the entire family.

As night falls, Raymonda, alone, falls into a troubled sleep. The statue of the White Lady comes alive and beckons Raymonda to join her to visit a magic garden of fantasies. It is in this garden that she sees her beloved Jean de Brienne, and the two lovers are wild with joy.

Suddenly the vision of Jean de Brienne changes into an Arab Sheik. Raymonda is confused and frightened as the Sheik confesses his great love for her. Raymonda faints and the vision disappears.

As dawn breaks over the horizon, Raymonda awakens, but is still troubled by this horrible nightmare. Thus ends **Act One.**

Act Two opens with a big party going on at the de Doris Palace. Mighty guests from all over the world have assembled. The most sumptuous is the Saracen Sheik Abderakhman with his huge entourage. Suddenly Raymonda recognizes Abderakhman as the man in her dreams!

Abderakhman follows her everywhere and offers her riches, gifts and power in exchange for her hand in marriage. Trying to convince her, Abderakhman deploys his entourage to perform all kinds of exotic dances. The dances don't impress Raymonda at all, so Abderakhman, infuriated by this rejection, attempts to kidnap Raymonda.

At that very moment King Andrey II and his Knights return from the war. With them is Jean de Brienne, who is aghast at the scene of his beloved being kidnapped. The King sees a horrible situation developing and he proposes that Jean de Brienne and Abderakhman settle their differences with an honorable fight to the death. The duel takes place immediately and, thanks to the White Lady, de Brienne is the victor. So dramatic is the finale of the **Second Act** that many people think the ballet is over!

The **Third Act** takes place in Hungary where Jean de Brienne and his bride, Raymonda celebrate their wedding in the Royal Palace of King Andrey II. During the wedding celebration many different guests dance, thus enabling the virtuoso dancers to impress the audience.

The story takes place during the Middle Ages. The time of the Crusades. The opening scene is a birthday party at the palace of Countess Sibil de Doris in which Raymonda, the Countess' niece, is being honored.

Raymonda has been raised by the Countess. She is attended by her handmaidens.

Raymonda is loved and respected by everyone because of her merry and carefree spirit.

The happy lovers dance with complete abandonment. Soon all their friends join in the dance.

Jean de Brien joins in the general merriment. He is joyful even though he knows he must soon leave for war.

As he dances with his beloved Raymonda, Jean de Brien hears the sound of the fanfares in the background. It is the rallying sound for all the troops to assemble.

The dance slowly comes to an end as the lovers' parting duet manifests the elegance, grace and courage of this noble knight.

The last moments before his departure are spent alone . . . the two lovers desperately sad. de Brien presents Raymonda with a silken scarf . . . thus ends the first scene of Act 1.

Raymonda is alone now and each touch of the silken scarf reminds her of her fiance Jean de Brien. How she longs for
him.

It's getting dark and Raymonda dreams of the war. The statue of the White Lady, protectoress of the Palace and the entire family of de Doris, comes to life in Raymonda's dream.

The White Lady takes Raymonda to a mysterious garden filled with fantastic creatures.

The fairy garden is a transformed reflection of Raymonda's thoughts. Everything that took place during the daytime reappears in her dreams. The dancing fairies represent Raymonda's friends dancing at the de Doris Castle.

In her dreams, Raymonda dances with her fiancé whom she found in this magic garden. Oh, what a happy dance!

The duet of the lovers is magnificent, ending with a wonderful show of love and affection.

Quite suddenly the vision changes to that of an Arab sheik. Thus ends Act 1.

Jean de Brien is still away at war when, sometime much later, an unexpected guest appears at the castle of Countess de Doris. This Saracen knight is Abderakhman. He has come to see Raymonda for himself since her beauty is known all over the world. He promises anything for her hand in marriage.

Raymonda is puzzled as she recognizes Abderakhman as the man in her dream.

In accordance with etiquette, Raymonda and her handmaidens dance with Abderakhman and the troubadours. Abderakhman falls to his knees, completely captivated with Raymonda. He asks her to dance (facing page) and promises her the world if she will only marry him.

Then the troubadours dance in front of Abderakhman, one by one (also facing page).

Raymonda's handmaidens join in and her closest friend (facing page) also dances before Abderakhman.

The Sheik offers dances from his whole entourage, but they do not seem to please Raymonda.

So the Sheik himself starts dancing.

Raymonda has never seen such a passionate dance.

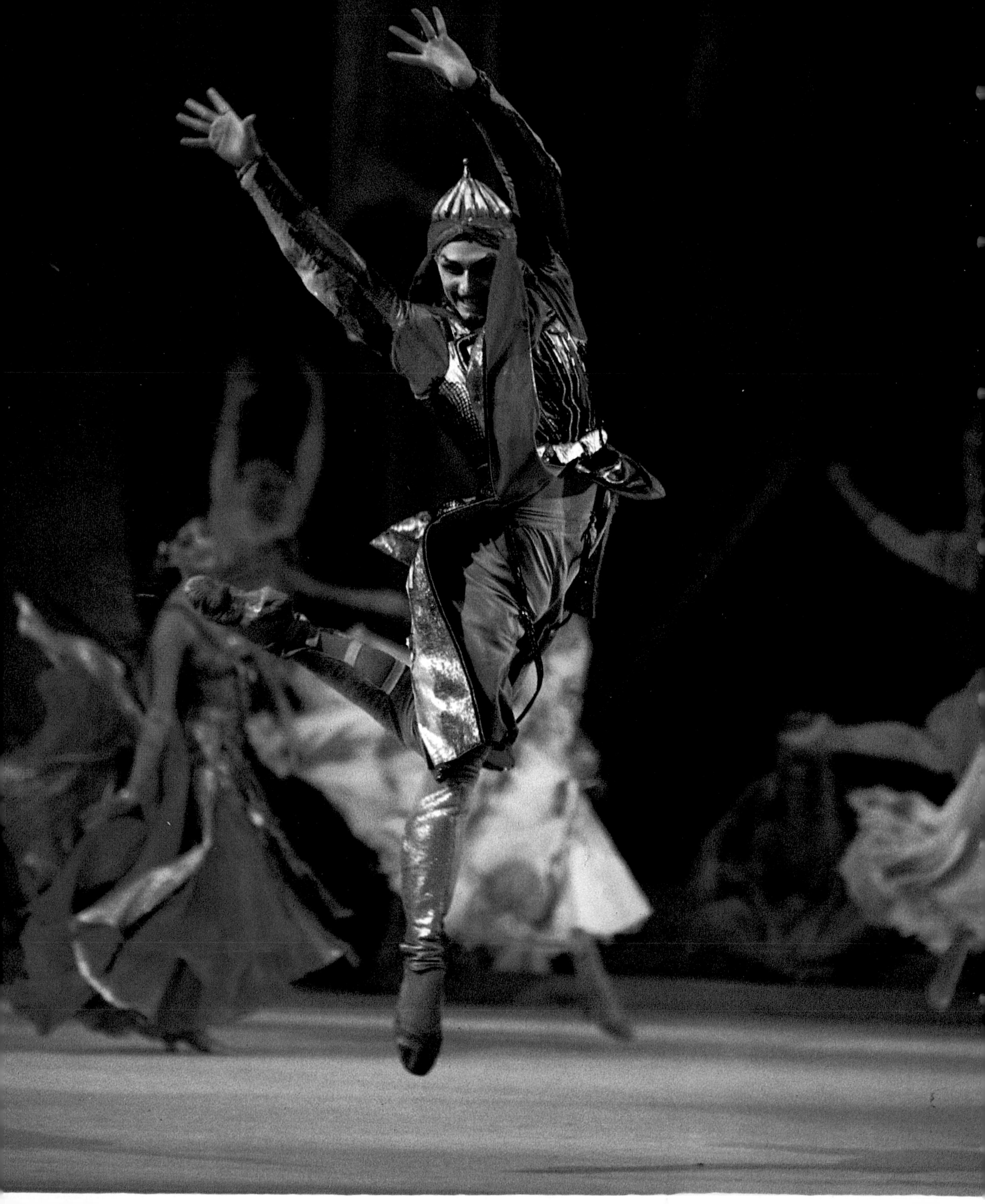

Various Oriental dances, never before seen in the West, are performed by the Sheik's entourage.

Finally the whole entourage performs a special dance for Raymonda. Won't anything the Sheik does impress her?

Finally the whole entourage beseeches Raymonda to consider their Sheik. But to no avail.

This rejection infuriates the Sheik. He is not accustomed to having his wishes ignored. In desperation he tries to kidnap Raymonda.

But at that very moment Jean de Brien returns from the war. He is aghast at what he sees. The King, who is also present, orders that a duel to the death is the best way to settle the problem.

The Saracen Sheik and the Crusader Jean de Brien fight for the hand of Raymonda.

The Sheik is mortally wounded.

Using his last bit of life, the Sheik crawls to the feet of Raymonda and dies professing his undying love.

Raymonda and Jean de Brien (facing page) are re-united.

Their reunification dance becomes very loving and warm. Thus ends Act 2.

The scene is the wedding party in Hungary where King Andrey II acts as host. The first dance is a Polish mazurka.

Everyone joins in the elegant mazurka.

Special Hungarian guests dance Hungarian dances. These famous dances have come down through the ages for us.

More and more dancers join in the Hungarian dancing.

Raymonda's best girlfriend joins in the Hungarian dancing, too.

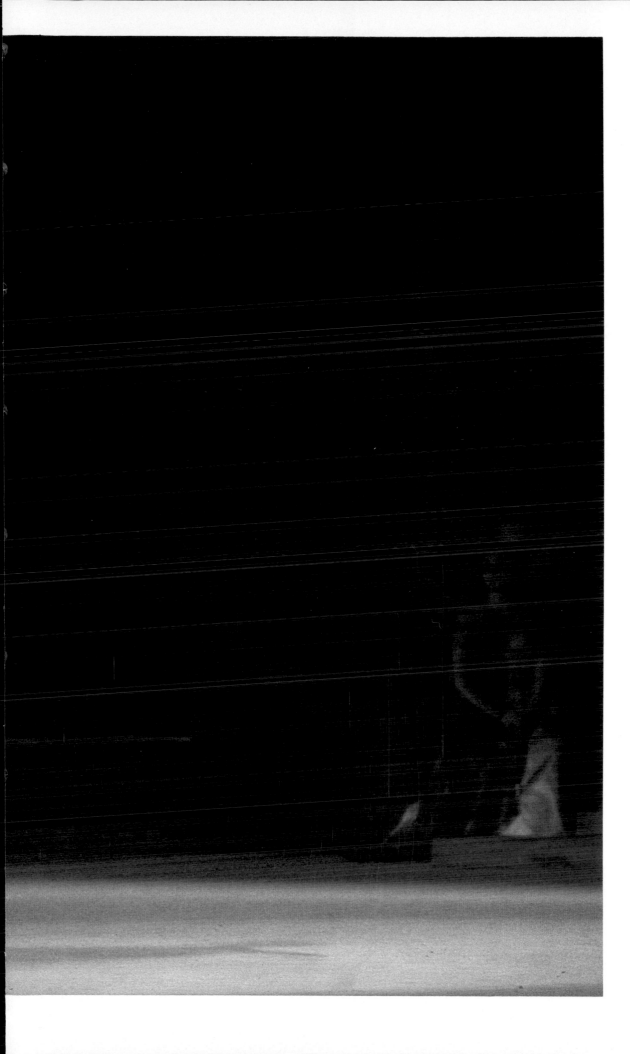

Even the troubadours are brought in to show their talents and to enliven the wedding party.

Then the bride and groom join (above and below) in dancing a Hungarian Grand Pas.

The hearts of the lovers, full of cheerfulness and happiness, are openly displayed in the dance which combines Hungarian dancing with accepted classical movements.

Harmony comes to the lovers as everyone dances.

The lovers, (facing page) continue dancing until Jean de Brien (above) declares his devotion to defend Raymonda the rest of his life.

Raymonda is thrilled with her wedding promises from Jean and she performs (also facing page) a special wedding dance.

As her wedding dance continues . . .

104

Jean de Brien comes flying in on wings of happiness.

Jean de Brien performs his own wedding dance.

The consummation of the wedding; everyone is dressed in white for this great occasion. Thus ends our story as the future promises happiness forevermore.

Supplementary Information About the Color Photographs

THE AUTHORIZED BOLSHOI BALLET BOOK OF

RAYMONDA